Servings with Love

Main Course Foods from which to choose

by Elizabeth Pistole

with daughters

Cynthia Poikonen and Carole Bagwell

ISBN No. ISBN 0-87162-222-X

Table of Contents

A few years ago I felt the usual ego-trip experience when my cookbook was published. *Food and Fellowship in the Christian Home* was fun to do and gave me a great deal of satisfaction to know that it included both recipes for tasty foods and hints for zesty living. I want this new edition to be more of the same. It is time, however, to edit and update. Some recipes are too time-consuming. Grandma's scrapple isn't too popular and newer dishes of quiche and eggplant Parmesan need to be included. I hope it will be a fun book for you as you explore it for new ideas of entertaining, smile at the antics and sayings of children or consider fasting to get rid of poundage after the holidays. I especially like the slogans and quotes at the bottom of the recipe pages.

The joyous element in redoing this book has been that my daughters, Cindy and Carole are coauthors with me. They were little when I wrote the first one. Now they are married to Carl Poikonen and Tim Bagwell and have established homes of their own. They are both excellent cooks and it is now my pleasure to visit them and sit around their tables and partake of delicious food and fellowship with them. They have each done

a yeoman job of making this book what it is. They have both shared many of their favorite recipes. Cindy gathered recipes from famous places, showed us ways of entertaining, and located regional food specialties. Carole gave ideas for page dividers, shared her school children's unique sayings and helped us understand the ways of measuring, especially with the new metric system. They have both shared with their memories of "when they were little." Since they are both elementary school teachers they share with us ways to manage the entertainment on minimal time and effort.

Sons, David and John, have also contributed by bringing college friends home to share and try new recipes. We sometimes lose friends this way, too, when the experiment is too far out. David is really the experimenter in the kitchen and is an excellent chef. And John, well, John just loves to eat and pleases any cook with verbal appreciation.

My husband, Hollis, has to be the most patient man ever as I still attempt to do my own thing in the kitchen. His flattery will get him anything when he says as we are eating out, "You know this is second best to you, don't you."

Thank you for the opportunity to be a part of your world, and I hope that this indeed may be a gift of food and fun for you.

Entertaining at home is becoming more popular than ever before, but with so many women working at jobs outside the home, *casual* and *easy* are the key words. In the next few pages you'll find ideas for many types of entertaining. You can make these affairs as simple or as formal as time and money permit. Many times accent pieces in

your home can make a table look really special. Pretzel sticks in a small crock, a plant in a soup tureen, colored placemats and napkins, flowers picked in your garden (or wild ones found along the road such as Queen Ann's Lace, bachelor's buttons, or many others) all make a table look special. You do not need to spend a great deal of money on your entertaining—good food and your own personal touches all say "I care."

Entertain at times convenient for you and your friends. Don't feel that to entertain five couples it is necessary to have a sit-down dinner for twelve. Brunch at Ten o'clock Saturday morning or after church Sunday morning would be fun for a change. A "little supper" after the theater or church, or just a get together with good friends in the evening, is a little different way of entertaining.

My husband and I belong to a Gourmet Club that meets once a month. There are seven couples and we meet at a different home each month. The hostess is in charge of the menu and theme. She also provides the main course and then gives the recipes for the other courses to the gourmet members for them to prepare. This is a fun way to try other foods and a good opportunity to get together with friends.

The following recipes and menu planners are simple ideas. They are simply helps or suggestions for various forms of entertaining. Have fun, enjoy yourself and your company, and *bon apetite.*

Appetizers

Braunschweiger Ball

1 pound braunschweiger
1 clove garlic, crushed (or garlic salt)
½ t. basil
¼ cup minced onion
1 8-ounce package cream cheese,
   softened
⅛ t. Tabasco sauce
1 T. mayonnaise

Mix the first four ingredients together, mashing with a fork. Form in a ball shape and chill. Blend the remaining ingredients and spread over the braunschweiger ball. Refrigerate and garnish with fresh parsley.

Cheese Ball

Makes one large or two small balls.

1 8-ounce package cream cheese,
   softened
1 jar pimento spread
1 jar old English spread

½ cup shredded cheese, sharp
1 t. Worcestershire sauce
1 T. parsley flakes
1 t. garlic salt
dash Tabasco sauce
1 T. minced onion
salt and pepper to taste
crushed pecans

Combine the above ingredients and chill slightly. When chilled, roll into ball and then roll in crushed pecans. Top with an olive or maraschino cherry. Refrigerate.

Cheese Spread

Makes 2 cups.

4 cups sharp Cheddar cheese,
   shredded
⅔ cup mayonnaise
1 T. hot horseradish (may add more to
   taste)
dash of Tabasco sauce
salt and pepper to taste
crushed pecans

Combine shredded cheese, mayonnaise, horseradish, Tabasco, salt and pepper. Chill, then garnish with crushed nuts. This spread may be served with crackers. It also looks attractive served in a small crock.

Cheese Balls

1 heaping tablespoon salad dressing
8-ounce package cream cheese
grated cheese
1 wedge bleu cheese
½ cup finely cut celery
crushed nuts

Soften bleu cheese and blend with cream cheese and salad dressing. Add celery and some crushed nuts. Shape cheese mix into balls, allowing about 1 teaspoonful to each ball. Coat balls with grated cheese. Chill. Serve on toothpicks.

Cream Cheese Spread

Makes about 1½ cups.

1 8-ounce package cream cheese, softened
½ cup chopped dates
¼ cup chopped pecans
dash of lemon juice
½ cup drained, crushed pineapple
1 to 2 T. mayonnaise

Combine the above ingredients using as much mayonnaise as needed to make the mixture smooth. Good served with nut breads or spread on crackers.

Lusty Cheese Snack

1 2-pound box Velveeta cheese
1 cup mayonnaise
1 5-ounce jar horseradish
5 drops Tabasco sauce

Melt all the above ingredients in a double boiler. Pour into containers and chill.

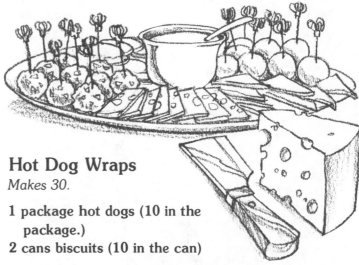

Hot Dog Wraps

Makes 30.

1 package hot dogs (10 in the package.)
2 cans biscuits (10 in the can)

Cut the hot dogs in thirds. Divide the biscuits in half and use the half to wrap around each hot dog. Place on a very lightly greased cookie or baking sheet and bake at 400° for 10 to 15 minutes or until browned. Serve with dips of mustard, catsup, or relish. Left over biscuits may be baked and used for breakfast.

Olive and Cheese Balls

Makes 45 to 50 balls.

½ pound cheddar cheese, grated
¼ cup butter, softened
¼ t. paprika
1 cup all-purpose flour
45 to 50 tiny stuffed drained Spanish
   olives

Preheat oven to 375°. Combine the cheese, paprika, and flour. Mix until the pieces of cheese disappear and it is deep yellow in color. Allow this mixture to stand at room temperature for about 15 minutes.

Pinch off a piece of dough (about 1 teaspoon) and flatten. Place a well-drained olive in the center and cover it completely with the cheese mixture. Place on an ungreased cookie sheet and chill 10 to 15 minutes to "set" the balls. Place in the oven and bake approximately 25 minutes or until lightly bowned. Serve hot.

Hot Dip

1 8-ounce package cream cheese
2 T. milk
¾ cup chopped dried beef
2 T. green pepper, chopped
⅛ t. pepper
2 T. minced onion
½ cup sour cream
¼ cup chopped nuts

Blend all the ingredients together—except for the nuts. Place in an 8-inch pie pan and sprinkle the nuts on top. Bake at 350° for 15 minutes. Serve with crackers, etc.

Guacamole

Makes about 2 cups.

1 medium tomato, peeled
2 ripe avocados
1 T. grated onion
a few drops of Tabasco (suit to taste)
a few drops of lemon juice
¼ to ⅓ cup mayonnaise

Mash tomato and avocado with fork until creamy. Add the remaining ingredients and mix well. Chill until ready to serve. This is good served with corn chips or assorted crackers.

Clam Dip

2 small cans minced clams
2 t. lemon juice
1 chopped onion
½ green pepper, chopped
¼ cup butter
oregano
paprika
dash pepper
¾ cup seasoned bread crumbs
1 slice American cheese

Drain clams, keeping ½ of the clam juice. Put clams in sauce pan with lemon juice. Heat. Put onion, green pepper and clam juice in blender. Mix until liquid, then put in sauce pan with clam mixture. Stir in bread crumbs and melted butter. Add dash of pepper and a dash of oregano. Put into small casserole dish and sprinkle with paprika before putting cheese slice on top. Bake at 350° for 15 minutes, or until bubbly.

Hot Crab Dip

Makes about 2 cups.

**1 8-ounce package cream cheese,
    softened**
¼ cup mayonnaise
¾ t. prepared mustard
1½ T. sauterne or white cooking wine

2 t. confectioners' sugar
¼ t. salt
dash of garlic salt
**1 can crab meat (about 6½ ounces)
    flaked and drained**

Combine all of the above ingredients except crab meat in a double boiler or at a low heat to avoid scorching. Heat until thoroughly blended, then add crab meat. Heat again. Serve hot with crackers or bread sticks.

Bleu Cheese Dip

1 package bleu cheese
½ cup sugar
½ cup vinegar
½ cup salad oil
1 T. garlic salt
1 T. Italian seasonings
1 T. dried vegetables
salt and pepper

Blend the above ingredients together. This is good served with raw vegetables (cauliflower, cherry tomatoes, carrots, celery, etc.) or as a salad dressing.

Frozen Fruit Slush

3 cups sugar
3 cups water
1 No. 2 can crushed pineapple
7 mashed bananas
1 small jar maraschino cherries
1 medium-sized can frozen orange
    juice
1 orange juice can of water

Heat sugar and water until dissolved. Cool completely. Mix fruits and juice and water into sugar/water mixture. Freeze at least 24 hours, stirring once each hour for the first 3 hours. Thaw about 1 hour before serving.

Cranberry-Orange Relish

Makes 1 quart.

All-sugar recipe
4 cups cranberries
2 oranges
2 cups sugar

No-sugar recipe
4 cups cranberries
2 oranges
1 cup marmalade or jelly
1 cup corn syrup

Put cranberries through food chopper. Quarter whole oranges, but do not peel. Remove seeds and put fruit through chopper. Add marmalade and corn syrup (or sugar) and mix well. Chill a few hours before serving.

Ham Puffs

Makes 24.

1 8-ounce package cream cheese,
    softened
1 t. minced onion
½ t. baking powder
1 egg yolk
dash of seasoned salt
24 bread rounds (toasted on one
    side)—or—cocktail party rye bread
    (also toasted)
2 cans deviled ham (about 2½ ounces
    each)

Mix the first five ingredients. Spread the untoasted sides of the bread with the ham. Cover each with the cheese mixture. Place on a baking or cookie sheet. Chill until the oven reaches the temperature of 400°. Bake 10 to 12 minutes.

A friend is a present you give yourself.

Crescent and Sausage Snacks

Makes 2 dozen.

8-ounce can crescent rolls
2 T. melted butter or margarine
¼ cup grated Parmesan cheese
1 to 2 t. oregano
8 brown-and-serve sausage links

Preheat oven to 375°. Separate crescent dough into 4 rectangles; press perforations to seal. Brush each with butter. Combine cheese and oregano; sprinkle over dough. Cut each rectangle crosswise to form 2 squares. Place a sausage link on each square; roll up. Cut each roll into 3 or 4 pieces; secure each with a toothpick. Place cut side down on an ungreased cookie sheet. Bake at 375° for 12 to 15 minutes until golden.

Holiday Appetizers

Serves 6

2 packages Smokies, cut into chunks
and browned
1 green pepper cut into squares
½ cup red maraschino cherries,
drained
1 can chunk pineapple, drained, but
save juice!*
5 t. corn starch

Take the pineapple juice (½ cup) and add 5 teaspoons corn starch to it. Bring to a boil and cook 5 minutes. Add the other ingredients and put in a chafing dish.

*   *Maple syrup may be added to the juice mixture.*

Party Meatballs

Serves 6 to 8 as an appetizer.

1 pound ground beef
½ cup dry bread crumbs
¼ cup minced onion
¼ cup milk
1 egg
1 T. parsley flakes (or substitute fresh
parsley)
1 t. salt
⅛ t. pepper
1 t. Worcestershire sauce
1 12-ounce bottle chili sauce
1 10-ounce jar grape jelly

Mix the above ingredients and form into small balls (approximately walnut size). Brown the meatballs in ¼ cup shortening. After they are browned remove from the heat (pour off any excess grease left in the pan). Mix 1 bottle (12 ounces) chili sauce and 1 jar (10 ounces) grape jelly. Heat the sauce then add the meatballs and simmer in the sauce for 30 minutes. Delicious!

Crab Appetizers

Makes 3½ dozen.

1 T. chopped onion
1 T. melted shortening
2½ T. flour
½ cup cream
1 cup crab meat
½ t. Worcestershire sauce
salt and pepper
½ cup dry bread crumbs

Cook onion in shortening until tender. Stir in flour; gradually add cream and cook, stirring constantly until the mixture thickens. Carefully remove all shell particles from crab meat and add meat to the white sauce along with the Worcestershire sauce. Salt and pepper to taste. Mix well and cool. When cool enough to handle, drop the mixture by teaspoonfuls into the bread crumbs and roll into small balls. Place in greased pan and broil, turning to brown all sides, or, if preferred, fry in deep fat (390°) about 2 minutes or until brown. Serve either hot or cold on toothpicks.

Nut Appetizers

A bowl of mixed nuts with raisins, or a bowl of Spanish peanuts with raisins make good "nibbles" before the main course is served. Also, sunflower or pumpkin seeds baked with a little butter and salt are good to nibble.

Party Mix

Yield 6¾ cups.

6 T. butter or margarine
4 t. Worcestershire sauce
1 t. seasoned salt—or—⅜ t. garlic
  powder and ⅜ t. salt
6 cups mixed dry cereal (mix wheat,
  corn, and rice cereals)
¾ cup salted nuts

Heat oven to 250°. Slowly melt butter in shallow pan. Stir in Worcestershire sauce and salt or substitute. Add cereal and nuts. Mix until all pieces are coated. Heat in over 45 minutes. Stir every 15 minutes. Spread on absorbent paper to cool.

Sharing is just giving a tiny part of yourself. It is related to touching another's life where you may happen to be. It may well be in the home, the neighborhood, your place of work or worship, or even the entire city. All it takes is to be aware and be willing to share. When we look around there are a multitude of ways it can be done. It doesn't take much to smile, send a card, or give a small gift of love from your garden or kitchen. No gift is too small for any occasion. It will give a little lift and may be a clue that you are discovering the happiness and joy of sharing. When do you give? Well, these times could be included:

—when the new baby comes home from the hospital.

—at a pitch-in dinner for those living in your block.

—for a birthday or an un-birthday.

—for anniversaries.

—when the teen-ager gets a driver's license.

—for a retirement.

—when the lawn mowing is finished.

—when going on a trip.

—for a change of jobs.

—for a graduation.

—at times of illness or death.

—for no reason at all, but just because you want to.

So go ahead. Act on your nudges and share something of yourself. A single rose from your garden, a telephone call, a homemade loaf of bread or cookies, a watermelon, a drive to the ice cream store, a "thinking of you" card—are all special gifts.

You hold them in your hand as an offering of friendship as you reach out and share. Someone has said it just right in this way:

Caring is the art of sharing.
Sharing is the art of living.
Living is the art of loving.
Loving is the art of caring!

COLD DRINKS

Apple Lemonade 18
Citrus Punch 19
Cranberry Punch 19
Egg Nog 17
Ice Cream Fruit Punch 20
Orange Apricot Nog 17
Orange Supreme 17
Orange Punch 20
Party Punch 19
Pink and White Cherry Punch 19

HOT DRINKS

Hot Buttered Tomato Juice 18
Hot Chocolate Mix 17
Hot Cider 18
Russian (Spiced) Tea 17

SUGAR

Beverages

Orange Apricot Nog

Serves 6.

1 orange, peeled and cut in small
   pieces
1 16-ounce can apricot halves,
   undrained and chilled
1 egg
½ cup cold milk
1 t. vanilla

Blend orange and apricots and juice in blender until smooth. Add egg, milk and vanilla. Blend one minute.

Egg Nog

1 quart milk
1 cup Eagle Brand sweetened
   condensed milk
2 eggs, beaten
½ T. vanilla
⅛ t. salt
1 pint whipping cream

Pour the other ingredients into the whipping cream.

Orange Supreme

Serves 6.

1 small can frozen orange juice
2 cans water
1 egg
1 pint ice cream or orange sherbet

Combine all ingredients in a food blender. Blend thoroughly and serve immediately as an appetizer with small crisp crackers or serve as a thirst quencher anytime.

Hot Chocolate Mix

1 8-ounce box instant milk
1 32-ounce box Nestle's Quik
1 11-ounce jar Coffee-mate
1 cup powdered sugar, sifted
1 cup granulated sugar
Add a few teaspoons cocoa.

Store in an airtight container. When ready to use add three tablespoons to a cup of hot water.

Russian (Spiced) Tea

1½ cups instant tea
1½ to 2 cups sugar (suit to taste)
2 cups Tang
1 large package dry lemonade mix (or
   about one cup if you use the can of
   dry mix)
2 t. cinnamon
1 t. cloves

Mix together and store in an airtight container. When ready to use add 2 to 4 teaspoons per cup of boiling water.

Hot Cider

1 gallon cider
¾ cup sugar
½ t. nutmeg
1 t. mint leaves
3 cinnamon sticks
3 oranges sliced and studded with
  cloves

Combine cider, sugar, and spices. Add the studded oranges and simmer being careful not to boil. The longer it simmers the better it will be.

Hot Buttered Tomato Juice
Serves 8.

1 46-ounce can tomato juice
1½ t. Worcestershire sauce
½ t. salt
½ t. oregano leaves
¼ cup butter

Combine all in saucepan. Cook over medium heat, stirring occasionally, until heated through (about 15 minutes). Serve piping hot.

Apple Lemonade
Makes 3 cups.

½ cup sugar
½ cup warm water
2 cups unsweetened apple juice
½ cup reconstituted lemon juice

In quart measure or pitcher, dissolve sugar in water. Stir in juices. Serve over ice cubes.

Some like them hot and some like them cold!

For *timesaving tips* use the frozen fruit juice concentrates, ready-to-serve eggnog, instant cocoa, or hot chocolate milk. For the *extra special touch* use molds for freezing colored water, ginger ale, or water with maraschino cherries or fruit slices. Place the mold with the fruit side up in the punch bowl. Fruit juice "ice cubes" are pretty, especially when mint leaves are frozen into the juice.

Pink and White Cherry Punch

Mix 2 quarts cold milk with ½ teaspoon almond extract and ½ cup maraschino cherry syrup. Add 1 quart of cherry-vanilla ice cream or 1 cup chopped maraschino cherries with vanilla ice cream.

Party Punch

To satisfy guests, place 4 tea bags in 1 quart boiling water, steep 10 minutes. Cool. Add 1 quart ginger ale, 1 large can pineapple juice, 1 large can orange juice. Sweeten to taste with brown sugar, white sugar, or white syrup.

When we worry we are playing God.
When we have concern we are used by God.

Cranberry Punch
Serves 16 to 20.

1 quart cranberry juice
1 can pineapple juice (1 quart)
1½ cups sugar
2 quarts ginger ale

Combine the first three ingredients above and when ready to serve add 2 quarts of ginger ale. You can make a festive ice ring out of Jello water, orange juice or anything that will mix with it. You may also add mint leaves if you wish. Using a Jello or juice base will keep the ice ring from diluting the punch when it melts.

Citrus Punch
Makes 12 to 15 servings.

1 6-ounce can frozen orange juice
1 6-ounce can frozen lemonade
1 6-ounce can frozen limeade
1 quart cold water
1 quart ginger ale

Combine all ingredients except ginger ale. Pour over ice block or cubes in bowl. Add ginger ale just before serving. Garnish with mint leaves if desired. Double the recipe to fill large punch bowl.

Ice Cream Fruit Punch

Makes 6 quarts or 48 punch-cup size servings.

6 cups of fruit juices—pineapple, orange, lemon or lime
3 cups sugar
9 cups water
1 quart ginger ale
1½ quarts sherbet or ice cream

Boil sugar and 4 cups water to dissolve sugar. Cool. Add fruit juice and remaining water. Chill. After putting it in the punch bowl, add the ginger ale and top with scoops of sherbet.

Orange Punch

Makes about 5 quarts of syrup.

Wash and cut 6 oranges. Squeeze juice and set aside. Grind rinds. Pour 2 quarts of boiling water over rinds, and let cool. Add 1 ounce of citric acid to orange juice. Drain liquid from rinds and to it add orange juice. Stir in 5 pounds sugar. Add a large can pineapple juice. To each quart of syrup, add 4 quarts of water.

Isn't it interesting that Jesus said in his Sermon on the Mount, "You are the salt of the earth; but if salt has lost its taste, how shall its saltness be restored?" (Matthew 5:13). All of the ingredients in our life may

be there but if we are not careful it is easy to become flat and dull. Life is too exciting for this to happen. Perhaps we should look at some spots that may cause us to grow weary in well-doing. Checklists and inventories are popular and are for us to spot-check, if we are honest, the trouble spots. And those small areas can become cancerous and insidiously creep into the rest of our lives until they contaminate both us and those with whom we live. Here we go. Do you—

—get adequate sleep and rest?
—postpone everything?
—look at criticism to see if it is valid?
—attempt to be teachable?
—express in love what you feel is right?
—misuse your feelings?
—constantly blame others?
—analyze those things that irk you?
—refuse to carry over anxieties from one day to the next?
—never admit that you were wrong?
—know that every job has some monotony?
—cultivate recreational activities and hobbies?
—stop and think?
—manipulate other people?
—feel like a martyr?
—remember to be grateful?
—do something for someone else?

"You shall know the truth, but first it will make you miserable."

Celebration is like a million candles lit with happiness and joy. It is reverence for life, It is saying thank you for the joy of being. It is transforming the daily events in our lives into something special. The day attains meaning and adds memory from events of other days. Celebration is taking the here and now, holding it to enjoy the lived moment, then letting it flow out from us to others. Celebration is the new insight of meaning that comes at unexpected moments. It is saying, "For all that has been, thanks; for all that is yet to be, yes!" (Dag Hammarskjold).

Take time in your day to be joyful. Celebrate! Celebrate! Celebrate! Be consciously aware of your day's events—events such as these:

—Holding hand with your husband as you walk together.
—Answering the phone and hearing one of the children say, "I just wanted to hear your voice."
—Fixing Norwegian pancakes as a special surprise.
—Lovingly putting strawberries, peaches, and corn in the freezer.
—Reaching your desired weight goal.
—Purchasing a new piece of furniture.
—Anticipating the first grandchild.
—Writing your friend a note to thank her for accepting you in spite of knowing you so well.
—Sincerely giving a compliment to someone.
—Looking "eyeball to eyeball" as you communicate.

—Seeing the church spire in the neighborhood.
—Daring to try something new or different.
—Planning for a trip.
—Making the shag rug an altar as you romp with the children.

Celebrate. Let your life be an inspiration, not a restraint; addition, not subtraction; wings, not a weight. Celebration with joy brings zest and sparkle to life. It is sunshine on the flowers; it is life more abundant; it is leaving the little narrow life behind. It brings bloom for faded hearts, rejuvenation for the prematurely old, and imagination for the dry, literal mind. Practicing celebration daily fires the soul with permanent enthusiasms. Celebrate and be joyful!

The personal touch is delightful, whatever hobby you have. Your own homemade method of keeping recipes reflects your personality. Since it is such a versatile preoccupation, you will want to keep a record of recipes as you collect them. List the name of the person, magazine, or cookbook from which you got the recipe, and any special comments. It is a good practice to date the recipe and the times and places you served it. Another notation might include the comments of those who were served the dish.

Some women prefer file folders for their recipes. Others insist that the loose-leaf notebook is the best way to keep them. Bound notebooks have the vote of many because the pages are not so easily torn out. Perhaps the most popular way of keeping recipes is the card file. Three-by-five- or four-by-six-inch cards are used most frequently. They can be lifted out and posted before you as you work. Dividers for classification of meats, pastries, and so on make it easier to find the recipes.

When one of your recipes proves to be especially popular, you may receive request for it. One way to give it to friends is by means of a personal recipe card. These cards are attractive and usually aren't too expensive. However you can buy plain cards, put a seal sticker in a corner and write your own "Here's what's cooking _____. Recipe from the kitchen of _____."

A most practical "place-card" at a Christmas dinner was a delightful gift I use constantly. It was made by the host—a four-inch square, one-inch thick foundation with a five-inch dowel stick on one side and a clothespin slanted at the top. It holds a recipe card so that it can be easily seen.

Soups

U.S. Senate Bean Soup

1½ cups dry great northern beans
water
1 smoked ham hock
1 medium potato, finely diced
1 clove garlic, minced
1 onion, diced
½ cup diced celery
salt, pepper
chopped parsley

Soak beans overnight in one quart water. For quick soak, bring beans and water to boil; boil 2 minutes. Cover; let stand 1 hour. Drain beans; measure liquid. Add enough water to make two quarts. Place soaked beans, water and ham hock in kettle. Cover; simmer 2 hours. Add potato, onion, celery, and garlic; simmer 1 hour. Remove ham hock; cut up meat. Remove 1 cup beans and some liquid; puree in blender. Return meat and pureed beans to soup. Heat. Season to taste with salt and pepper. Sprinkle with chopped parsley.

Summer Vegetable Soup

Makes about 2 quarts.

2 to 4 medium potatoes, peeled and
   diced
3 medium carrots, peeled and diced
salt
½ medium head cauliflower, diced
1 cup chopped spinach
1 T. flour
3 cups milk
1 T. butter or margarine
white pepper
few sprigs parsley, chopped

Bring 3 cups water to boil in kettle or Dutch oven. Add potatoes and carrots, season with salt to taste and bring again to boil. Cover and simmer about 10 minutes. Add cauliflower and spinach and cook about 5 minutes. Blend flour with a little of the milk and stir into hot mixture. Add butter and remaining milk and simmer about 10 minutes. Season with salt and white pepper to taste and sprinkle with parsley.

Canadian Cheese Soup

Yield: 2 quarts

¼ cup butter
½ cup onions, minced
¼ cup flour
1½ T. cornstarch
1 quart milk
1 quart stock
⅛ t. soda
½ cup carrots, diced
½ cup celery, diced
⅛ t. paprika
salt to taste
1 cup rarebit cheese or Old English
   cheese (cut in small cubes)
2 T. parsley, chopped

Melt butter and saute onions lightly. Add flour and cornstarch. Then add milk and stock, making a smooth white sauce. Add soda, vegetables, seasonings, and cheese cubes. Simmer for 15 minutes. Just before serving add the chopped parsley.

Life is not so short but there is time for courtesy.

Chicken Velvet Soup

Yield: 2½ quarts

¾ cup butter
¾ cup flour
1 cup warm milk
1 pint hot chicken stock
1 cup warm cream
1 quart chicken stock*
1½ cups chopped cooked chicken
¼ T. salt
dash of pepper

Blend well the butter and flour. Add milk, 1 pint of chicken stock, and cream; cook well. Add the remaining ingredients.

* *We use approximately 2½ quarts water to simmer one five-pound fowl— for stock.*

Ayres Tea Room, Indianapolis

For five cups of this delicious soup use:

6 T. butter or margarine
6 T. flour
½ cup milk
½ cup light cream
3 cups chicken broth
1 cup chicken
dash of pepper

Peanut Soup

Serves 6.

1 medium onion, chopped
2 ribs of celery, chopped
3 T. butter or margarine
2 T. flour
1 quart chicken broth
½ t. salt
pinch celery seed
1 cup smooth peanut butter
1 t. lemon juice
¾ cup milk
peanuts or sunflower seeds chopped

Saute the onion and celery in the butter. Cook 1 minute. Add 1 quart chicken broth, salt, and celery seed. Bring to a boil, then simmer 25 minutes. Add the peanut butter by blending in soup. Add lemon juice and milk. Serve with chopped peanuts or sunflower seeds.

French Onion Soup

4 to 6 servings.

4 large onions, sliced thin
2 T. margarine
4 cups brown stock (or use beef bouillon cubes)
1 t. Worcestershire sauce
2 hard rolls, sliced and toasted
grated Parmesan cheese

Cook onions in margarine until lightly browned. Add stock and Worcestershire sauce. Cook 20 minutes and season with salt and pepper. Sprinkle toast with cheese. Pour soup in bowls and float toast slices atop. Place under the broiler a few seconds until the cheese is lightly browned.

Hagerstown Onion Soup

6 T. margarine
4 T. flour
4 cups milk
2 cups chicken stock
1 cup chopped onion
½ t. salt
¼ t. pepper
¼ cup finely cut green onion
4 T. cream

Melt a little margarine in double boiler, add flour and mix well. Add milk and chicken stock and beat with wire whip to blend. Saute onion in 4 tablespoons margarine for 3 minutes. Add to soup mixture and cook 15 minutes. Add to rest of ingredients and serve.

If you don't know where you are going, you will probably end up somewhere else.

New England Clam Chowder

Makes 6 1½-cup servings.

¼ cup finely chopped salt pork
¾ cup coarsely chopped onion
2 cups diced potatoes
1 t. salt
⅛ t. pepper
2 7½-ounce cans minced clams or 1
    pint shucked fresh clams, diced
2 cups milk
1 cup light cream or undiluted
    evaporated milk
1 T. flour
2 T. milk

Cook salt pork in a heavy saucepan over moderate heat until crisp and brown. Cook onion in the fat until tender. Drain salt pork on paper towels. Add diced potatoes, salt and pepper, and liquid drained from the clams. Add water, if necessary, just to cover potatoes; cook over moderately low heat until potatoes are tender. Add clams. Stir in the 2 cups milk and cream; set aside for 2 hours. Reheat slowly over very low heat. Stir flour and the 2 tablespoons milk together to form a smooth paste. Stir into chowder and cook slowly over moderately low heat until slightly thickened. If possible allow chowder to stand in the refrigerator for 24 hours or longer before serving. Reheat when ready to serve and garnish with crisp pieces of salt pork.

She Crab Soup

2 cups white crab meat
1 pint milk
1 pint cream
¼ cup crab roe (or use 1 chopped egg
    yolk)
½ stick butter
⅛ t. pepper
⅛ t. mace
⅛ t. grated onion
Salt to taste
½ cup cracker crumbs

Put milk in double boiler with mace. Allow to simmer a few minutes. Add crab, roe (or yolk), butter, cream and cook 10 to 15 minutes. Thicken with ½ cup cracker crumbs. Season with salt, pepper, and onion.

FRUIT SALADS

LEAF SALADS

MEAT, BEAN, SHRIMP, POTATO SALADS

Salads

Heavenly Hash

Makes 6 servings.

Thoroughly mix 1 can (8¾ ounces) pineapple tidbits, well drained, 2 cups thawed Cool Whip, 1 cup coconut, 1 cup miniature marshmallows, ¼ cup chopped maraschino cherries, and 3 T. milk. Chill about 1 hour.

Orange Sherbet Salad

Serves 10.

2 3-ounce packages orange gelatin
2 cups boiling water
2 cans mandarin oranges drained and
   cut in half
¾ cup juice from oranges
1 pint orange sherbet

Dissolve gelatin in hot water; add juice from oranges and stir in orange sherbet. When mixture begins to set, add mandarin oranges. Chill until firm.

Sunny Lemon and Fruit Mold

2 3-ounce packages lemon Jello
1¾ cups boiling water
1¾ cups cold water
11-ounce can mandarin oranges,
   drained
⅓ cup maraschino cherries, quartered
1 banana, sliced
cream cheese, whipped

Dissolve Jello in boiling water. Add cold water. Chill until partially set. Fold in fruit. Pour into oiled 6-cup mold. Chill until firm. Unmold. Top with softened cream cheese.

Wilted Lettuce Salad

Makes 6 servings.

¾ pound bacon
1 large head leaf lettuce
1 medium onion, thinly sliced
¼ cup vinegar
1½ t. sugar
½ t. mustard
¼ t. salt
dash pepper

In a large skillet fry bacon slices until crisp. Drain. Reserve ¼ cup bacon drippings.

Tear lettuce into bite-sized pieces and put into salad bowl. Crumble the bacon and mix with the onion. Toss until well mixed.

Stir remaining ingredients into the bacon drippings (¼ cup). Heat to boiling stirring constantly. Remove from heat and immediately add to the lettuce mixture. Toss until the lettuce is slightly wilted and coated with dressing.

You have touched me—I have grown.

Boiled Salad Dressing

2 T. butter
1 T. flour
2 eggs
1 cup vinegar
2 t. sugar
1 t. dry mustard
⅔ t. salt
⅓ pepper

Put butter, flour, sugar, eggs, mustard, salt, and pepper into a bowl or the top part of a double boiler and cook over hot water till they begin to thicken. Add vinegar and continue cooking three minutes. Beat mixture occasionally while cooling. Keep in a cool dark place. This dressing will remain good several weeks.

Apricot-Pineapple Salad

2 boxes orange gelatin
2 cups hot water
1 cup combined fruit juice
1 large can apricots, cut in small
  pieces
1 medium can crushed pineapple
1 cup miniature marshmallows
½ cup sugar
3 T. flour
1 cup combined fruit juices
1 egg, beaten
½ pint whipped cream
grated cheese

Mix gelatin, hot water, and fruit juice. Chill liquid. Add apricots, pineapple, and marshmallows. Chill until set. Combine sugar, flour, fruit juices, and beaten egg. Cook until thick. Cool. Fold 1 cup of whipped cream into this mixture. Spread over Jello and sprinkle grated cheese on top.

Tomorrow's Salad

2 eggs
¼ cup sugar
¼ cup vinegar
2 T. butter
2 cups miniature marshmallows
2 cups diced pineapple
¼ cup maraschino cherries
2 cups white cherries
1 orange, diced
1 cup heavy cream, whipped

Beat eggs; add sugar and vinegar. Cook over low heat until thick and smooth. Remove from heat and stir in butter. Pit cherries; dice pineapple, cherries, and orange and mix together with vinegar dressing. Fold in whipped cream and let stand in refrigerator 24 hours.

Cranberry Fluff

Makes 8 to 10 servings.

2 cups raw cranberries, ground
3 cups miniature marshmallows
¾ cup sugar
2 cups diced unpared apples
½ cup seedless green grapes
⅓ cup broken walnuts
¼ t. salt
1 cup heavy cream, whipped
lettuce

Combine cranberries, marshmallows, and sugar. Cover and chill overnight. Add apples, grapes, walnuts, and salt. Fold in whipped cream. Chill. Spoon into individual lettuce cups.

Cherry (Strawberry) Salad

1 21-ounce can pie filling, either
    cherry or strawberry
1 can Eagle Brand sweetened
    condensed milk
1 cup miniature marshmallows
1 cup nuts
1 large container Cool Whip

Mix all ingredients by hand. Freeze in a 9-by-13-inch baking dish. Serve by cutting into small squares and placing on lettuce leaves.

Six-Cup Salad

1 cup sour cream
1 cup nuts
1 cup coconut
1 cup marshmallows
1 cup mandarin oranges
1 cup pineapple chunks

Mix ingredients together lightly. Can be served immediately or keeps well if made ahead of time. Serve with crackers.

Pineapple-Cheese Salad

Serves 4 to 6.

1 package lemon gelatin
1 cup hot water
1 cup pineapple juice
1 cup crushed pineapple
¼ cup maraschino cherries
1 8-ounce package of cream cheese

Dissolve gelatin in hot water. Add pineapple juice and chill. Mix with cheese 2 tablespoons cherry juice or cream. When smooth, combine cheese with crushed pineapple and chopped cherries. When gelatin begins to thicken, add salad mixture. Pour into mold and chill until firm. Unmold on lettuce and garnish with mayonnaise and olives.

Avocado-Citrus Salad

2 ripe avocados
lemon juice
salt
2 oranges
2 grapefruit
Bibb lettuce

Cut avocados in half crosswise; remove pits. Peal each half; cut into ¼-inch slices. Sprinkle slices with lemon juice and salt. Pare and section oranges and grapefruit. Arrange avocado slices and fruit sections on Bibb lettuce on salad plates. Serve with a French or your favorite dressing.

Frozen Fruit Salad

⅓ cup chopped nuts
3 T. chopped maraschino cherries, drained well
1 9-ounce can crushed pineapple, drained
1 pint sour cream
¾ cup sugar
2 T. lemon juice
⅓ t. salt
1 banana, diced

Combine ingredients and stir together gently but well. Spoon into one dozen paper muffin pan liners. Freeze. Remove paper before serving.

Coke and Bing Cherry Salad
Serves 16.

1 large can crushed pineapple
1 large can Bing cherries
1 can pecans
2 small bottles Coca-Cola (12 ounce total)
1 8-ounce package cream cheese
2 packages cherry gelatin

Drain fruit. Heat juice from fruit and enough water to make 2 cups liquid. Dissolve gelatin. Cool. Add chopped cherried, nuts, cream cheese, cold Coke and pineapple. Chill until set.

Pretzel Salad

8-ounce package pretzels (crushed)
3 T. sugar
¾ cup margarine, melted
1 8-ounce package cream cheese, softened
1 cup sugar
small container whipped topping, thawed
1 6-ounce package strawberry gelatin
2 cups boiling water
1 16-ounce package frozen strawberries

Mix the pretzels, sugar and melted margarine together. Press into a 9x13-inch pan. Bake for 10 minutes at 350°. Cool.

Cream together the cream cheese, sugar, and whipped topping. Spread over the cooled pretzel crust. Chill. Mix gelatin and boiling water; stir until gelatin is dissolved. Add frozen strawberries. Stir until soft set. Add to crust and cream cheese mixture. Chill until ready to serve.

Jacque's Chicken Salad

Serves 3 or 4.

1 10-ounce package frozen French-style green beens, cooked and drained
½ cup Italian salad dressing

Combine beans and Italian dressing. Chill several hours, stirring occasionally.

3 large split chicken breasts, cooked, deboned and chilled
½ cup mayonnaise
¼ cup whipping cream, whipped
1 cup diced celery
2 t. drained capers, if desired
3 lettuce leafs
6 tomato slices
6 ripe olives
2 hard cooked eggs, quartered.

Cut three thin slices from chicken breasts. Reserve. Fold chicken, celery, ½ t. salt and dash papper into mayonnaise mixture. Chill well.

Place lettuce on platter. Spoon chicken salad into lettuce. Arrange reserved chicken slices and dollops of mayonnaise atop; sprinkle with capers. Drain green beans; arrange around lettuce. Garnish with tomatoes, olives and egg wedges.

Easy Does It Salad

Serves 4 to 6.

1 medium-sized carton Cool Whip
1 medium can of crushed pineapple, drained
1 medium-sized carton cottage cheese
1 3-ounce package Jello, dry—either red or green in color

Simply mix all the ingredients by hand, and refrigerate until ready to serve by the spoonfuls.

Lettuce Surprise Salad

1 head lettuce
1 head cauliflower
1 onion
1 cup mayonnaise
½ cup Parmesan cheese
1 pound crisp, crumbled bacon
salt and pepper

Chop lettuce and cauliflower into small flowerettes. Chop onion finely. Mix these three ingredients and put into a bowl. Add one cup mayonnaise on top of mixture. Add Parmesan cheese and bacon—DO NOT MIX! Sprinkle with salt and pepper. Cover tightly. Refrigerate overnight. Mix when ready to serve.

Modern Caesar Salad

Makes 6 to 8 servings.

½ cup salad oil
¼ cup red wine vinegar
1 large clove garlic, crushed
2 t. Worcestershire sauce
¼ t. salt
dash pepper
3 slices bread, cubed
½ cup shredded Parmesan cheese
1 ounce blue cheese, crumbled (¼ cup)
8 cups torn lettuce (about 1 medium head) or romaine
1 egg

For dressing, shake together salad oil, vinegar, garlic, Worcestershire sauce, salt, and pepper in screw-top jar. Refrigerate a few hours or overnight to blend flavors. Toast bread cubes in slow oven (225°) for 2 hours. (Commercial bread cubes may be substituted.)

To serve, sprinkle cheese over lettuce in salad bowl; add toasted bread cubes. Shake egg well with dressing; toss lightly with salad.

Lettuce Surprise (Pea Salad)

Shred one head of lettuce on the bottom of an 8-by-12-inch glass dish.

Add a layer of chopped green onions (about 6).

Add a layer of chopped celery (about 1 cup).

Add a small package of frozen peas—cooked, dried, and cooled.

Sprinkle 2 T. sugar over peas.

Add two cups of mayonnaise.

Cover tightly and refrigerate. Do not stir. Pass at the table and let each one "dip" his or her own amount. May be adapted with 1 cup French onion dip; sprinkle with Parmesan cheese or crumbled bacon.

Korean Salad

1 large package fresh spinach (cut veins out and chop large pieces)

5 strips of crisp bacon, crumbled

1 can chilled, drained bean sprouts

1 can water chestnuts, drained, sliced thin

3 hard-cooked eggs, diced

Dressing:
1 cup oil
¼ cup vinegar
⅓ cup catsup
1 T. Worcestershire sauce
¾ cup sugar
salt and pepper to taste

Mix all the salad ingredients together in a large bowl. This makes a "big" salad. Combine the dressing ingredients together in a jar and store in the refrigerator until ready to use. Add as much dressing as desired right before serving. The dressing makes more than is necessary for this salad and will be good on any green salad.

Christiana Campbell's Salmagundi

8 servings.

salad greens (vary according to your
    family's preference but make
    enough to serve 8)
1 pound Virginia ham, thinly sliced
    and cut into strips
1 pound chicken or turkey, thinly
    sliced and cut into strips
4 hard-cooked eggs, sliced
16 sweet gherkins
8 celery hearts
16 sardines
16 anchovy fillets
oil and vinegar dressing

*Arrange the greens on individual salad
plates or on a large platter. Place
remaining ingredients evenly over the
top and around the greens. Sprinkle
lightly with oil and vinegar dressing.*

Raggedy Ann Salad

Recipe makes an individual serving.

half a hard-boiled egg, cut lengthwise
1 T. shredded carrot
half of small tomato
2 small sweet pickles (gherkins)
2 lettuce leaves
1 portion crabmeat or tuna fish salad
    (consisting of fish, chopped celery,
    and mayonnaise)
cloves for eyes and nose
narrow strip of pimiento for mouth

*Place egg at top (yolk-side down);
arrange shredded carrot around egg to
represent hair; make face on egg with
cloves and pimiento. Below egg, place
half tomato, round side up, for body;
place pickles horizontally at each side of
tomato (arms); at bottom of tomato,
place fish salad; over salad, arrange
lettuce leaves to resemble skirt.*

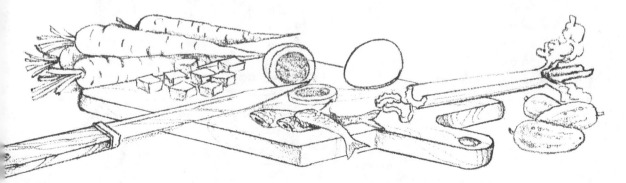

Louis Pappas' Greek Salad

6 medium potatoes, cooked and peeled
2 medium onions, sliced
¼ cup finely chopped parsley
2 medium green peppers
salt to taste
½ cup favorite salad dressing
1 large head lettuce, shredded
watercress
2 medium tomatoes, each cut into 6
    wedges
1 medium cucumber, peeled and cut
    lengthwise into 8 fingers
1 medium avocado, peeled and cut
    into wedges
8 ounces feta cheese, cut into fingers
4 canned beets, sliced
8 large shrimp, shelled, deveined, and
    cooked
4 anchovy fillets
12 ripe olives
12 medium hot preserved peppers
4 radishes, cut into roses
4 scallions
½ cup white vinegar
⅛ cup olive oil
¼ cup vegetable oil
oregano

Prepare potato salad: Slice potatoes into mixing bowl. Add onions and parsley. Cut 1 of the green peppers into thin slices; add to potatoes. Sprinkle lightly with salt. Add salad dressing; toss lightly. Chill while preparing rest of ingredients.

Cut remaining green pepper into rings. Just before serving arrange lettuce and watercress on large serving dish. Start building a mound by placing potato salad in center of lettuce. Add alternate layers of tomatoes, cucumber, avocado and cheese. Garnish with green pepper rings, beets, shrimp, anchovies, olives, hot peppers, radishes, and scallions. Prepare dresssing: In bowl blend vinegar, olive oil, vegetable oil. Sprinkle over salad; sprinkle oregano on top.

Twenty-Four-Hour Bean Salad

Serves 12.

1 15½-ounce can cut wax beans
1 16-ounce can French-style green
  beans
1 17-ounce can kidney beans
1 cup thinly sliced onions
½ cup cider vinegar
½ cup granulated sugar
½ t. salt
¼ t. pepper
½ cup salad oil

Day before serving, combine all beans, drained, with onions. Combine oil, vinegar, sugar, salt, and pepper in jar; shake well until blended. Pour over beans; cover and refrigerate until served, tossing occasionally.

To serve, drain dressing from bean mixture and pile beans lightly on lettuce or chicory on salad dish.

Potato Salad

6 diced potatoes
  (well cooked and still warm)
1 medium-sized onion, diced fine
1 cup diced celery
1 cup diced sweet pickles
¼ cup vinegar
¼ cup sweet pickle juice
1 cup mayonnaise
2 T. prepared hot horseradish
3 T. sugar
dash of pepper
dash of salt

Blend ingredients in the order given. Blending and mixing well while potatoes are still warm makes this salad creamy. Sprinkle lightly with paprika and center with sprig of celery.

German Potato Salad

¼ cup light vinegar
2 T. sugar
pepper to taste
few celery leaves, chopped fine
1 small onion
3 T. water
1 t. salt
small amount of celery seed
6 potatoes
¼ pound bacon

Cook potatoes and cut in any style you like. Fry slightly the bacon and onion. Mix ingredients together and pour over potatoes and mix. A sweet red or green pepper may be sliced fine to add color and flavor. If a large amount is needed, the seasonings should be doubled or tripled, according to the amount of potatoes used.

We in the United States are among a group of 5 percent of the world's peoples who do not use the metric system of measurement. Instead, we use an outdated hodgepodge of units that we are comfortable with only because we learned it as children, and not because it is a well-ordered, logical system. But the day of our conversion to the international system (metric) is not too distant. For years business and industry have used metrics, but now we are seeing metric weights and measures in cookbooks and on food packages. What does it mean to us?

First, don't throw away your favorite recipes and cookbooks. You can keep using them as you do now.

Second, for metric recipes now appearing, purchase measuring spoons and cups, many of which are dually marked with standard and metric graduations.

Third, try to "think metric" and avoid making comparisons between the two systems. However, for beginners, a few basic comparisons may help to accustom you to the new system. For example: A *liter* is two ounces more than a quart; a *meter* is a little longer than a yard; a *gram* is a little heavier than a paper clip and a *kilogram* is slightly heavier than two pounds.

The *hot dog,* definitely a symbol of Americana, was born at a ball game. Legend has it that Harry Stevens, who owned the refreshment concession at the New York Polo Grounds, needed a warm food to serve to the cold fans. The most practical, he decided, were sausages. His salesmen sold the frankfurters in the stands by yelling, "Get your red hot dachshund sausages here." Sportswriter Tad Dorgan heard the cry and was inspired to create a talking sausage as a cartoon character. Because he couldn't spell dachshund, he named his creation "hot dog." The cartoon character has long since faded, but the name has stuck.

In the strictest interpretation of the word, *lasagna* is the wide noodle that is used in many types of Italian dishes. We Americans, however, use the word to refer to a casserole made with lasagna noodles, cheese, and meat sauce. No matter how the word is used, it means delicious eating.

A very old Italian story tells of the mother who would measure her children's mouths to know how wide to make the noodles. Nowadays most of us do it the easy way and buy them at the grocery store!

The summer of 1873 was so hot and dry that in California's San Joaquin Valley the grapes dried on the vines. One enterprising grower, refusing to see a year's work wasted, shipped the dried grapes to a grocer friend in San Francisco. The grocer, equally as enterprising, marketed them as "Peruvian delicacies" simply because a ship from Peru was in port at the time. The promotion was such a success that it inspired the beginnings of the *raisin* industry!

In the seventeenth and eighteenth centuries, good *home-cured hams* could be found in every colony, but those of Virginia and Maryland were special. There the hogs were fed on mast—a mixture of fruits from the persimmon, beech, chinquapin, chestnut, hickory, and oak trees.

Today, Smithfield hams are the most famous of all country-style hams. To be eligible for the Smithfield name a ham must be cured, given a heavy smoke, and be aged as long as a year within the city limits of Smithfield, Virginia. And the hogs must be fed on peanuts. Unlike most hams today, country-style hams must be cooked before eating.

Hot cross buns began in early Greek and Roman times. These currant-filled buns were symbolic of the sun and bisected by a cross into the four seasons. Later in history, these little buns with their cross became associated with Easter so exclusively that they were sold only on Good Friday. Now it isn't necessary to wait for the holiday. The English brought their recipe for hot cross buns to the United States, and now they can be eaten and enjoyed anytime.

Vegetables

Copper Carrot Pennies

2 to 2½ pounds cooked carrots, sliced
1 diced green pepper
1 diced onion
1 can tomato soup
1 t. mustard
1 t. Worcestershire sauce
½ cup oil
Dressing:
1 cup sugar
¾ cup vinegar
salt
pepper

Refrigerate 24 hours before serving.

Cheese Grits

4 cups boiling water
1 t. salt
1 cup grits
1 stick butter
4 ounces garlic cheese
2 eggs, beaten, measured with milk to
   make 1 cup

Preheat oven to 350°. Cook grits in water and salt. While hot add butter and cheese. Cool slightly. Add egg mixture. Place in buttered deep casserole and bake for 30 minutes.

Scalloped Cabbage

Serves 6.

5 cups shredded raw cabbage
2 cups medium white sauce
1 cup grated cheese
2 T. fine crumbs

Mix cabbage and white sauce in 1½-quart baking dish. Top with grated cheese and crumbs. Bake in moderately hot oven 400° about 20 minutes, until tender.

Corn Pudding

2 cups cream-style corn
2 eggs, well beaten
1 t. sugar
1 t. salt
¼ t. pepper
1 T. butter
4 T. cracker crumbs

Heat oven to 350°. Mix ingredients except cracker crumbs and pour into baking dish. Cover with crumbs and bake for 1 hour.

True friendship is a plant of slow growth.

Scalloped Tomatoes

1 1-pound can tomatoes
1 small can tomato puree
½ t. salt
½ to 1 cup brown sugar (depending on taste)
2 cups brown bread crumbs
½ cup margarine

Combine the tomatoes, puree, salt, and brown sugar. Put the crumbs and butter on top. Bake at 350° for 30 minutes.

Scalloped Asparagus

2 cans asparagus spears
1½ cups seasoned white sauce
Ritz crackers
butter

Mix asparagus and white sauce. Cover with buttered Ritz cracker crumbs. Bake at 325° until golden brown and bubbly.

Hungarian Noodles

4 ounces fine noodles, cooked according to directions and then rinsed
1 cup cream-style cottage cheese
1 cup dairy sour cream
¼ cup finely chopped onion
1 clove garlic minced
1 T. Worcestershire sauce
dash Tabasco sauce
1 T. poppy seeds
½ t. salt
dash pepper

Mix all the ingredients and put in a greased pan and bake for 25 to 30 minutes at 350°. Sprinkle with Parmesan cheese and paprika a few minutes before removing from the oven.

Green Bean Casserole

2 cans green beans
1 can cream of mushroom soup
3 T. milk
grated cheese or French fried onion rings

Dilute soup with milk. Mix drained green beans with soup. Top with cheese or onion rings and bake at 350° about 30 minutes.

Vermont Baked Beans

Makes 6 to 8 servings.

2 pounds dried yellow-eye beans (or
  pea beans)
4 t. salt
½ pound lean salt pork
1 cup maple syrup
2 t. dry mustard
1 t. baking soda

*Wash the beans and soak them
overnight in enough water to cover
them. Drain; place in a kettle, cover with
water, and bring slowly to a boil. Simmer
for 30 minutes. A few minutes before
removing from heat, stir in baking soda.
Drain beans. Score salt pork and place
half in a heavy baking dish. Cover with
the beans. Combine maple syrup and
mustard; blend with one cup boiling
water and pour over the beans. Put the
second piece of salt pork on the top of
the beans. Add just enough boiling water
to cover the beans. Bake in a preheated
over (350°) for 6 hours. About 30
minutes before the beans are done
remove the cover so they can brown a
little.*

Sweet Potato Casserole

3 cups mashed sweet potatoes
1 t. vanilla
¾ cup sugar
2 eggs
⅓ cup melted margarine

*Mix the above ingredients together. Then
put the mixture into a baking dish.*

1 cup brown sugar
½ cup coconut
1 cup nuts (optional)
⅓ cup flour
⅓ cup melted butter

*Mix these ingredients together and put
on the sweet potato mixture as a
topping. Bake for 30 minutes at 350°.*

Broccoli with Stuffing

2 packages frozen broccoli
2 eggs, beaten
1 onion, chopped fine
1 can mushroom soup
½ cup mayonnaise
1 cup grated Cheddar cheese
¼ cup melted margarine
½ package herbed stuffing mix

Cook broccoli. Combine eggs, onion, soup, and mayonnaise. Place a layer of broccoli in a 2-quart casserole. Add a layer of cheese. Pour half of the sauce on top of broccoli and cheese. Repeat layers until all the ingredients are used. Top with the stuffing mix. Sprinkle the margarine on top. Bake for 30 minutes at 350°.

Vegetable Casserole

2 packages chopped broccoli
1 package baby lima beans

Cook and drain (according to directions). Mix the vegetables together and put into a casserole.

1 can mushroom soup
1 cup sour cream
1 package onion soup
1 can water chestnuts, sliced
1 stick butter (or margarine) melted

Layer the above ingredients (do not mix) and top with 2 cups Rice Krispies. Cover with foil and bake at 350° for 30 minutes.

Old Stone Inn Scalloped Zucchini

4 large zucchini, cut into round slices
  ½ inch wide
4 hard-cooked eggs, chopped
1 10¾-ounce can condensed Cheddar
  cheese soup
⅓ cup heavy cream
½ cup grated sharp Cheddar cheese
¼ cup flavored dry bread crumbs

Layer zucchini and eggs alternately in a greased 8-inch square pan. The top layer should be eggs. Mix soup and cream; spoon evenly over casserole. Sprinkle top with cheese and bread crumbs. Bake in a preheated 350° oven for 40 to 45 minutes, or until zucchini is easily pierced with a fork and the top of the casserole is lightly browned.

Broccoli Casserole

2 T. margarine
1 small onion, diced
½ cup diced celery
1 cup rice
1 small jar of Cheese Whiz
1 can cream of mushroom soup
2 packages chopped frozen broccoli
  (thawed)

Saute onion and celery in margarine. Meanwhile cook rice according to directions on box. Combine rice and sauted vegetables. Add cheese and soup and thawed broccoli. Bake at 350° for 45 minutes in a 9x13-inch baking dish.

Scalloped Potatoes

4 cups pared thin sliced potatoes
1 t. salt
⅛ tsp. pepper
Milk
2 T. butter
1 can cream of chicken soup
1 T. flour

Put ½ of potatoes in greased baking dish, 1⅓ quart size. Combine salt, pepper, and flour. Sprinkle part of this over potatoes and dot with butter. Repeat with this procedure. Measure soup and add enough milk to make 2 cups liquid. Pour over potatoes. Cover and bake for 30 minutes at 350°. Remove cover and bake until done. Cheese may be added on top the last 10-15 minutes before they are done.

Eggplant Parmesan
Serves 3 to 4.

1 medium eggplant (about 1 pound)
1 t. salt
¼ cup flour
½ t. salt
¼ t. pepper
½ cup vegetable oil
½ cup chopped onion
½ cup chopped green pepper
1 large clove garlic, minced
1 8-ounce can tomato sauce
½ t. leaf oregano
1 8-ounce package mozzarella cheese,
  sliced
¼ cup Parmesan cheese

Pare and cut eggplant into 8 slices, ½ to ¾ inch thick. Sprinkle both sides of eggplant slices lightly with the 1 teaspoon salt. Place between paper toweling; weigh down with a heavy plate and let stand for 30 minutes. Rinse off slices well and dry on paper toweling. Combine flour, ½ teaspoon salt and pepper on piece of waxed paper. Coat eggplant slices on both sides with the flour mixture. Pour 2 tablespoons of the oil in a large skillet; saute eggplant slices, a few at a time, adding more oil as needed. When lightly browned on both sides drain the slices on paper toweling. Add to the skillet remaining oil, onion, green pepper, and garlic. Saute over low heat for five minutes, stirring frequently. Add tomato sauce and oregano; simmer 5 minutes. Spoon one half the tomato sauce mixture into a 1½-quart shallow baking dish. Arrange eggplant slices on the sauce. Cover with slices of mozzarella and spoon remaining sauce on top. Sprinkle with the Parmesan cheese. Bake at 350° for 30 minutes.

Fried Corn

Remove corn from the cob and put in large heavy skillet. Add enough butter to cook the corn without sticking. Cook until corn begins to get done then add just enough milk to make a gravy-like mixture. Continue cooking at a higher heat for about 5 minutes. Lower the heat and simmer for about 20 minutes or until the mixture thickens and most of the milk has been absorbed. Season to taste with salt and pepper.

Fried Rice Almondine

6 T. oil
1 cup blanched, split almonds
1 medium onion, chopped
1 medium green pepper, chopped
1 t. garlic salt
½ t. pepper
4 cups cooked rice (cooled)
4 T. soy sauce

Put oil in skillet; add almonds and cook over low heat stirring until lightly browned. Stir in onion, green pepper, and seasonings. Cook five minutes. Add rice and soy sauce. Mix well and cook 10 minutes or until well heated.

Corn Fritters

1 cup flour, sifted
1½ t. baking powder
1 T. sugar
1 scant t. salt
1 egg
¼ cup milk
½ cup whole kernel corn, canned
deep fat for frying

Resift flour, baking powder, sugar and salt together. Add egg, milk, and corn and stir until well blended. Bring deep fat to 350° and then drop batter into fat by the teaspoonful. Fry until golden brown, turning once to cook evenly. Place on serving platter and sprinkle with confectioner's sugar. Makes about 16 fritters.

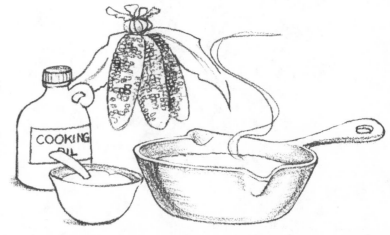

Once again it is summer and we need a change of pace as well as scenery. One busy mother after a long winter of busy activities said:

I feed the cat and feed the dog.
I feed the cow, I feed the hog.
I feed the kids, I feed the turks;
Some day I think I'll ditch the works!

We do need to look at something besides the kitchen stove and sink. We need firelight, moonlight, and sunlight! We need tramping and lazing around. We need time for our souls to catch up with our bodies as we whiff the good woodsmoke of a campfire. We need fun, food, and fellowship in the out-of-doors. We need to see the shimmer of a lake and to lean quietly against a tree. We need to sing, on or off key, when the meal is over. (Well, I guess we need it.)

In planning for the "blue-sky" meals think primarily of simplicity and variety. Avoid elaborateness or fanciness, but include colorful and attractive servings. The rule-of-thumb need is for sweet and tart tastes as well as crisp and soft textures in the meal.

You will have more time for relaxing if you
—don't forget the matches.
—use old pans.
—avoid easily perishable foods.
—keep foods covered until needed.
—be patient with the out-of-door insects.
—be like "Smokey the Bear" if you have a fire.
—gaze for long moments at something specific, like a cloud, a blade of grass, or a leaf.
—breathe deeply.
—have fun!
—take time to smell the flowers along the way.

If liberation is so great, why is it that even when man helps in the home, woman's work still is never done?

The "new woman" and changing family roles reflect significant issues which must be looked at objectively as the traditional male-female roles are reexamined. Is there a proper place for women? Arguments and heated discussions flow from one extreme of the movement for women's liberation to the other side, the "total woman" advocates. Regardless of the position of women, it is understood that change is coming—gradually and deliberately, and improvement *is* becoming measurable in a number of areas. New spheres of influence for women can be observed in education, politics, vocations (both secular and religious), and social relations. Definitely, the working woman is here to stay. "Times are a'changing" and as we look at the facts we need to remain flexible and open to new situations. Women believe that they are entitled to equal social, professional, and legal rights, and the stirrings and rumblings of discontent are fast increasing in volume and deafening din. The struggle is bringing about a change in attitude as well as in behavior. Some stereotypes are slowly giving way. Sexism is being eliminated from textbooks and personality traits are being looked upon as "human" rather than peculiarly male or female. Boldness, initiative, and courage are coming to be praised in both men and women. Gentleness, compassion, and sensitivity are to be admired in both sexes.

Somewhere between the extremes are the majority of women, who are searching for their own roles. Some persons have the answers worked out intellectually and feel good about who they are and what they are about. Yet the double bind for many is that emotionally they cannot accept without guilt that which they know is right for them. Women who choose not to work outside the home should not be defensive. Full-time homemakers need not apologize. Yet it is equally true that women who work outside the home may find real joy in homemaking, though they give a smaller proportion of their attention to doing so. Either-or choices need not be demanded. True liberation for a woman is not an "outrage" but a door through which she may enter into areas of greater fulfillment and a more positive and creative relationship with herself and others. Every human being should be able to be what she or he wants to be, to exercise potential to the very fullest, and to use his or her God-given gifts in the best way. Then all humankind will benefit.

Main Dishes

Fried Steak with Cream Gravy

1 pound round steak, cut about ½ inch
   thick
flour
1 t. salt
¼ t. pepper
3 T. salad oil
1 cup milk
3 cups hot mashed potato

With 3 tablespoons flour, salt and pepper, sprinkle both sides of steak. With a mallet (or the side of a saucer works well) pound the steak until the flour disappears; cut into four pieces and fry over a high heat in hot oil. Cook 3 to 5 minutes until well browned and of desired doneness. Keep warm on a warmed platter or in the oven.

In the same skillet stir 2 tablespoons of flour into pan drippings until well blended. Gradually stir ½ cup water into the flour mixture, stirring and scraping until all the brown "particles" are loosened from the pan. Add milk and stir constantly until the gravy is smooth and thick. Serve the steak with the gravy and mashed potatoes.

Elegant Oven Stew
Serves 4 to 5.

2 pounds round steak, cut into 1-inch
   cubes
2 cups sliced carrots
1 cup sliced celery
2 medium onions, sliced
1 can water chestnuts, drained and
   sliced
1 can sliced mushrooms, drained
3 T. flour
1 T. sugar
1 T. salt
1 16-ounce can tomatoes
1 cup beef bouillon

Mix first 6 ingredients in Dutch oven or crockpot. Then mix next 3 ingredients and stir into meat mixture. Finally add bouillon and tomatoes. Cover tightly and cook in a 325° oven or on top of stove for 4 hours. In crockpot cook 6 to 8 hours on high.

Look toward the light, and the shadow of your burden will fall behind you.

New England Boiled Dinner

4 pounds corned beef brisket
6 small beets, cleaned
6 medium turnips, diced
8 small onions, peeled
8 carrots, cleaned
1 small head cabbage, cut in sixths
6 medium-sized potatoes, peeled

Place beef in a large kettle or dutch oven. Cover the meat with cold water. Bring to a boil and then boil 15 minutes; skim off the top. Reduce heat and simmer 3 to 4 hours, or until meat is tender. In the last hour of cooking add beets, turnips, carrots, cabbage, and onions. Add potatoes in the last half hour of cooking. Take the skins off the beets before serving. Arrange the meat on a large platter and surround with vegetables.

Italian Spaghetti

Serves 4 to 6.

1 pound ground beef
1 can tomato soup
1 can Italian tomato paste
1 cup water
1 large onion, chopped
1 green pepper, chopped
½ t. black pepper
1 pound spaghetti
1 t. salt
1 t. sugar
½ t. garlic salt
2 t. chili powder
2 T. Worcestershire sauce
2 T. Italian grated cheese

Saute onion, pepper, and ground beef. Add tomato soup, paste, and other ingredients. Let cook slowly for two hours or more. All ingredients can be added more or less according to taste. Pour over hot cooked spaghetti.

Experience is the name everyone gives to their mistakes.

Cube Steaks Parmesan

1 egg
½ cup buttermilk
1¼ t. salt
½ t. pepper
¼ t. oregano
3 T. chopped onion
1¼ cups dry bread crumbs
½ cup Parmesan cheese
6 cube steaks
½ cup cooking oil
2 8-ounce cans tomato sauce
½ t. sugar

Combine egg, buttermilk, salt, pepper, oregano, and onion; mix well. Mix dry bread crumbs with ¼ cup of cheese. Dip steaks in egg mixture, then in crumb mixture and brown in heavy skillet in cooking oil. When steaks are brown on both sides, add tomato sauce to which the sugar has been added and top with remaining cheese. Bake uncovered in a 325° oven for 25 minutes.

Pasties

1 to 1½ pounds round steak
1 good-sized onion
5 medium potatoes
5 medium carrots—optional
2 bay leaves (finely crushed)
salt and pepper to taste
5 strips uncooked bacon
1 recipe pie crust (enough for 2 crust pie)

Pound steak and cut into 1-inch cubes. Roll in flour and brown with a few pieces of onion in hot fat. Chop vegetables into very small cubes and mix with steak in a large mixing bowl. Add salt, pepper, and bay leaf. Roll pie crust into five ovals. Put steak mixture into center of crust and place uncooked bacon strip on top. Fold crust over mixture to form a half-moon shape. Bake in 350° oven for 45 minutes or until done.

La Fonda's Chili Con Carne

Serves 4 to 6.

2 T. vegetable shortening
2 pounds coarsely ground lean chuck
2 cloves garlic, mashed
1½ t. crumbled oregano
2 T. flour
2 11-ounce cans condensed chili beef
   soup
1 10½-ounce can condensed beef
   broth
½ cup diced pimiento
salt

Heat shortening in a deep saucepan. Add beef and cook until meat is crumbly and well browned. Add garlic, oregano, and flour. Stir to blend. Add chili beef soup, beef broth, and pimiento. Stir to blend and heat until bubbly. Season to taste with salt.

Deep Dish Pizza

1 pound ground beef
¼ cup chopped onion
1 1-pound can tomatoes
¼ cup chopped pepper
1 package cheese pizza mix
1 12-ounce package mozzarella cheese

Brown meat, pepper, and onion. Drain. Stir in tomatoes, pizza sauce and spices (if included in pizza mix). If spices are not included add your own to taste (oregano, and so forth). Simmer 15 minutes. Heat oven to 425°. Prepare pizza dough as on the package. Press the dough onto the bottom and halfway up the sides of greased 13x9x2-inch pan. Cover with half of cheese and meat sauce. Repeat the layers and sprinkle with Parmesan cheese. Bake 20 to 25 minutes.

Beef Barbecue

Combine:
1 small bottle catsup
1 small bottle chili sauce
6 T. mustard
1 T. vinegar
2 T. Worcestershire sauce
3 to 4 T. brown sugar
2 to 3 small onions, chopped bay leaf
5 to 6 pounds chuck roast

Pour sauce over the onions and chuck roast. Cook covered in the oven for at least 4 hours at 300°. Flake and serve on buns. You could use a crockpot.

Pizza Bread

French bread
pizza sauce (homemade or use a
    ready-made)
1 pound hamburger, browned and
    crumbed
mozarella cheese (shredded)

Lightly butter the bread (cutting lengthwise so the pieces are longer), then spoon on the sauce, next add the cheese, and last the meat. Bake at 350° for 15 or 20 minutes. These can be made ahead and heated just before serving.

Suzette's Casserole

8 ounces elbow macaroni
½ cup butter or margarine
2 medium onions, finely chopped
1 green pepper, chopped
2 pounds ground beef
1 clove garlic, crushed
3 8-ounce cans tomato sauce
1 small can whole-kernel corn, drained
1 small can mushrooms, drained
1 T. brown sugar
1 T. chili powder
1 T. Worcestershire sauce
2 t. salt
dash of pepper

Cook the macaroni according to package directions. Grease a 3-quart casserole. Melt the butter or margarine in a skillet and saute the onions and green pepper until translucent. Add the ground beef and garlic; cook until the meat is browned. Drain any excess grease from the meat, then stir in the remaining ingredients. Put the meat mixture into the casserole and then add the macaroni. Cover. Refrigerate overnight to allow flavors to blend. Bake in a 325° oven for 90 minutes.

Meat 'n' Pepper Corn Bread

1 T. shortening
½ cup chopped onion
1 pound ground beef
1 8-ounce can tomato sauce
½ t. chili powder
1 t. salt
¼ t. pepper
1 recipe corn bread
7 or 8 pepper rings.

Lightly brown beef and onion in skillet, using shortening. Add tomato sauce and seasonings and simmer while preparing corn bread. Arrange the green pepper rings in a design in the bottom of a heavy skillet. Pour the meat mixture over the pepper rings, and then put the corn bread (made without sugar) on top. Bake 20 to 25 minutes at 425°.

Sour Beef for Potato Dumplings

3 pounds beef cubed
1½ cups vinegar
2 cups water
1 large onion
1 t. mixed whole spices (including bay leaf)
1 t. salt
⅛ t. pepper

Combine the above ingredients in a large bowl and set in refrigerator over night. Remove meat and brown in 1 tablespoon hot fat. Return to the other ingredients and simmer for 2 to 2½ hours, or until tender.

Fifteen minutes before serving, soften 10 or 12 ginger snaps in a cup of water. Add to liquid and boil to make gravy. Serve over potato dumplings.

Spaghetti Pie

Serves 6.

6 ounces spaghetti
2 T. margarine
½ cup grated Parmesan cheese
2 well-beaten eggs
1 pound ground beef

¼ cup chopped onion
¼ cup chopped green pepper
1 cup canned tomatoes, cut up
1 6-ounce can tomato paste
½ to 1 t. salt
1 t. sugar
1 t. oregano
½ t. garlic salt
1 cup cottage cheese
½ cup shredded mozzarella cheese

Cook the spaghetti according to package directions (should be a little over 3 cups). After draining the spaghetti add the margarine. Stir in the Parmesan cheese and eggs. Form the spaghetti mixture into a "crust" in a buttered 10-inch pie plate. Cook the ground beef, onion, and pepper until meat is browned and vegetables tender. Drain. Add undrained tomatoes, tomato paste, sugar, oregano, and garlic salt. Heat and cook 10 to 15 minutes. Spread the cottage cheese over the bottom of the "crust." Fill with the meat and tomato mixture. Bake uncovered at 350° for 20 minutes. Sprinkle the mozzarella cheese on top and bake 5 minutes longer.

Lasagna

Makes 12 servings.

½ pound Italian sausage
½ pound ground beef
1 T. basil
1½ t. salt
1 1-pound can tomatoes
2 6-ounce cans tomato paste
10 ounces lasagna noodles
3 cups creamy cottage cheese
½ cup grated Parmesan cheese
2 T. parsley flakes
2 beaten eggs
1 t. salt
½ t. pepper
1 pound mozzarella cheese, sliced very
  thin

Brown meat slowly and drain off excess fat. Add the next five ingredients. Simmer 20 to 25 minutes (uncovered), stirring occasionally.

Cook noodles according to package directions. Drain and rinse.

Combine the remaining ingredients except the mozzarella cheese.

Place half the noodles in a 13x9x2-inch baking dish; spread with half the cottage cheese filling; add half the mozzarella cheese and half the meat sauce. Repeat layers.

Bake at 375° for about 30 minutes. Let the lasagna stand for 10 minutes before cutting into squares.

Chow Mein Hot Dish

1 to 1½ pounds hamburger
1 large onion, diced
1 can chicken-rice soup
1 can mushroom soup
2 cans water
½ cup uncooked rice
1 cup celery, diced
3 T. soy sauce
1 small can mushrooms

Brown hamburger and diced onion. Mix with remaining ingredients and bake 1 hour at 350°. Last 15 minutes: sprinkle Chinese noodles on top.

Stuffed Peppers

10 medium-sized peppers
1½ pounds lean hamburger
2 or 3 T. or ½ stick butter
1 medium onion, minced
1 cup rice (before cooking)
1 No. 303 can tomatoes
salt and pepper to taste

Boil rice until almost tender. Wash all the starch out so it won't be sticky.

Brown meat in skillet. Add the onions, saute 5 minutes, pour in rice, tomatoes, salt, and pepper. Cook about 2 minutes.

Wash peppers and cut tops off carefully; save tops for covers. Stuff peppers and replace the tops. Arrange in baking pan. Add 1½ cups of water. Bake 1 hour at 350°. Baste peppers occasionally with pan juice. Serve hot.

Swedish Meatballs

Makes 6 to 8 servings.

1 pound ground beef
½ pound ground pork
½ cup minced onion
¾ cup fine dry bread crumbs
1 T. minced parsley
1½ t. salt
⅛ t. Worcestershire sauce
1 egg
½ cup milk

Thoroughly mix the above ingredients. Shape mixture into balls the size of a walnut. Brown in ¼ cup hot fat. Remove from heat and stir into the fat:

¼ cup flour
1 t. paprika
⅛ t. pepper
½ t. salt

Stir in 2 cups boiling water and ¾ cup sour cream. Return meat to gravy and cook for 15 to 20 minutes.

Instant Tacos

1 pound ground beef
1 can chili without beans
1 package Fritos

Brown meat lightly in skillet. Add chili and simmer until thoroughly blended. Place handful of Fritos in cereal bowl and cover with meat mixture. Serve piping hot!

Pepper Steak

2 to 2½ pounds sirloin (cut into thin strips)
2 medium onions (cut into rings)
2 green peppers (cut into rings)
1 1-pound can stewed tomatoes
3 small cans mushroom steak sauce
1 8-ounce can tomato sauce
2 small jars sliced mushrooms
1 T. oregano
1 basil leaf

Season the meat (salt and pepper) and brown quickly in one stick margarine. Add the onions and peppers. Cook until translucent. Add the remaining ingredients and simmer for 30 minutes. Serve over rice.

Shish Kebab

1½ pound round steak—cut in
   1½-inch cubes

Combine the following ingredients. Add the meat and stir to coat. Refrigerate several hours or overnight, turning meat occasionally.

½ cup cooking oil
¼ cup lemon juice
1 t. salt
1 t. dried marjoram
1 t. dried thyme
½ t. pepper
1 clove garlic, minced
½ cup chopped onion
¼ cup snipped parsley

Fil! 4 to 6 skewers with meat and vegetables alternately. Vegetables which may be used would be green peppers, quartered tomatoes or cherry tomatoes, fresh mushrooms, cooked whole onions, canned small boiled potatoes, chunks of zuchinni, and so on.

Broil over hot coals 10 to 12 minutes, turning and brushing often with marinade.

There can be no rainbow without a cloud and a storm.

Sicilian Meat Roll

Serves 8 to 10.

2 beaten eggs
¾ cup soft bread crumbs
½ cup tomato juice
2 T. parsley
½ t. oregano
¼ t. each salt and pepper
1 clove garlic, minced
2 pounds ground beef
8 thin slices boiled ham
6 ounces shredded mozzarella cheese

Combine first 7 ingredients. Add the ground beef and mix well. On waxed paper or foil pat meat to a 12x10-inch rectangle. Arrange ham slices on top, leaving small margin around edges. Sprinkle cheese over ham. Roll up meat and place seam side down in a 13x9-inch pan. Bake at 350° for 1¼ hours. Put some cheese wedges over top of roll and return to oven until melted.

Eat yourselves full,
but clean your plates empty.
—Amish

Hamburger Stroganoff

Serves 4 to 6.

½ cup minced onion
1 clove garlic, minced
¼ cup butter
1 pound ground beef
2 T. flour
1 t. salt
¼ t. pepper
1 pound fresh mushrooms, sliced, or 1 8-ounce can sliced mushrooms, drained
1 10½-ounce can cream of chicken soup
1 cup sour cream
parsley

Saute onion and garlic in butter over medium heat. Stir in meat and brown. Drain most of the fat off. Stir in flour, salt, pepper, and mushrooms. Cook 5 minutes. Stir in soup. Simmer uncovered 10 minutes. Stir in sour cream. Heat through. Garnish with parsley. Serve over noodles.

Trader Vic's Baked Chicken Cashew

2 whole chicken breasts, about 1½ pounds, split
4 chicken thighs, about 1 pound
2 T. salad oil
2 T. butter or margarine
1 10½-ounce can condensed cream of chicken soup
⅓ cup sour cream
1 T. chopped onion
½ t. paprika
generous dash pepper
½ t. monosodium glutamate (MSG)
½ cup coarsely chopped cashews

In skillet, brown chicken in oil and butter; pour off fat. Remove chicken. Stir to loosen browned bits. Blend in remaining ingredients except cashews; add chicken. Cover; cook over low heat 45 minutes, stirring now and then. Add cashews; cook 15 minutes more. Cook uncovered to thicken the sauce, if desired.

Every meal shared in love is a feast.

Chicken a la Can Can

Serves 6.

1 10½-ounce can condensed cream of chicken soup
1 10½-ounce can condensed cream of celery soup
1 soup can of water
½ cup celery
1 12-ounce can boned chicken or 1½ cups boned, cooked chicken pieces
1⅓ cups instant rice
1 3½-ounce can French fried onions

Combine the soups, water, celery, and chicken. Add instant rice, right from the box. Stir in mix. Bring quickly to a boil. Cover and reduce heat. Simmer about 7 minutes. Put in casserole, top with onions and put in slow oven for 15 to 20 minutes until onions are heated.

Pimiento-Mushroom Sauce

1 can condensed cream of mushroom soup
1 cup dairy sour cream
¼ cup milk
¼ cup chopped pimiento

Combine ingredients; heat, stirring, until hot. Do not let mixture boil.

Chicken and Biscuit Pie

1 1-pound can of chicken in gravy
1 can condensed cream of chicken
  soup
1 T. instant onion or 1 small diced
  onion
1 8-ounce can of peas
1 3-ounce can of mushrooms
1 package refrigerator biscuits

Mix chicken in gravy, soup, and seasonings. Add drained peas and mushrooms. Heat slowly, stirring now and then, until bubbling hot; turn into a 1½-quart casserole. Arrange the biscuits on top of the casserole and bake in a hot oven (425°) for about 15 minutes, or until biscuits are done.

Savory Crescent Chicken Squares
Makes 4 servings.

3-ounce package softened cream
  cheese
2 T. melted margarine
2 cups cooked, cubed chicken
¼ t. salt
dash of pepper
1 T. chives
2 T. milk
1 T. chopped pimento

Mix the above ingredients together. Separate an 8-ounce can of crescent rolls into 4 triangles. Seal the perforations. Spoon ½ cup chicken mixture onto the center of each rectangle; pull the 4 corners of the dough to the center of the mixture. Seal and brush the tops with 1 tablespoon melted margarine. Sprinkle the tops with crushed croutons. Bake on an ungreased cookie sheet for 20 to 25 minutes until golden brown. Refrigerate any leftovers.

Hot Chicken Salad

2 cups cooked chicken
2 cups chopped celery
1½ cups slivered almonds
2 t. grated onion
½ cup grated cheese
½ t. prepared mustard
½ t. salt
2 T. lemon juice
1 cup mayonnaise
1 cup crushed potato chips

Mix celery, chicken, almonds, onion, mustard and salt in bowl. Add lemon juice to mayonnaise. Fold into chicken mixture. Turn into greased casserole and sprinkle with crushed potato chips. Bake at 350° for 30 minutes.

Company Chicken Ring

Serves 6.

¼ cup butter or margarine
½ cup flour
1 t. salt
3 cups chicken stock
½ cup milk
1 t. lemon juice
pepper to taste
paprika
3 cups diced, cooked chicken
½ cup sliced stuffed olives
2 T. chopped pimiento
½ t. poultry seasoning

Melt butter and stir in flour. Add salt, stock, and milk. Cook over low heat till thick, stirring constantly. Add remaining ingredients. Heat. Serve in center of biscuit ring.

Biscuit rings: Sift together 1½ cups flour, 3 teaspoons baking powder, ¾ teaspoon salt, and ½ teaspoon poultry seasoning. Cut in ¼ cup shortening. Stir in ½ cup plus 2 tablespoons milk. Bake in greased 8-inch ring mold in hot oven (450°) for 15 minutes. Turn onto hot serving plate. Brush with butter and fill with hot chicken.

Chicken Parmesan

Serves 6

6 chicken thighs or 3 breasts, boned and skinned
1 egg
¼ cup water
1 cup fine, dry bread crumbs
¼ cup salad oil
3 8-ounce cans tomato sauce
½ t. basil
½ t. oregano
¼ t. thyme
¼ cup Parmesan cheese
4 ounces mozzarella cheese

Flatten chicken thighs or breasts by rounding between 2 pieces of waxed paper. Beat egg with water in a shallow dish. Dip chicken in egg mixture and coat with crumbs. In a large skillet heat oil, add chicken, and brown on both sides. Mix tomato sauce and spices. Spread a thin layer of sauce on bottom of a 1½-quart glass baking dish. Place chicken over sauce, overlapping slightly. Cover with rest of sauce; sprinkle with Parmesan. Bake in 400° oven for 30 minutes. Place a slice of mozzarella on each piece and return to oven until cheese melts—about 5 minutes.

Chicken 'n' Stuffing Scallop

3½ cups herb-seasoned stuffing
3 cups cubed cooked or canned
   chicken
½ cup butter or margarine
½ cup flour
¼ t. salt
dash of pepper
4 cups chicken broth
6 eggs, slightly beaten

Prepare stuffing according to package directions for dry stuffing. Spread in a 13x9x2-inch baking dish and top with chicken.

In a large saucepan, melt butter; blend in flour and seasonings. Add cool broth; cook and stir until mixture thickens. Stir small amount of hot mixture into eggs, return to hot mixture, pour over chicken. Bake in 325° oven for 40 to 45 minutes, or until knife inserted halfway to center comes out clean. Let stand 5 minutes to set; cut in squares and serve with pimiento-mushroom sauce.

Buttermilk Fried Chicken

1 frying chicken, cut up
1 small onion, cut up
salt and pepper to taste
1 cup or more buttermilk
shortening and flour

Salt and pepper chicken, dip in buttermilk, then in flour. Dip in buttermilk again, then in flour again. Fry in very hot fat until brown. Remove chicken from fat. Brown flour for gravy. Add onion and simmer about 1 minute. Add ½ to ¾ cup of buttermilk and enough water to make the gravy as thick as you like it. Put chicken back into gravy and pressure cook for 5 minutes. Let cool normally, and remove chicken from gravy and serve.

Never let yesterday use up today.

Chicken Tetrazzini
Serves 6.

¼ cup butter or margarine
¼ cup flour
½ t. salt
¼ t. pepper
1 cup chicken broth
1 cup whipping cream
1 8-ounce package spaghetti, cooked
  and drained
2 cups cubed, cooked chicken
1 3-ounce can mushrooms, drained
½ cup grated Parmesan cheese

Heat oven to 350°. Melt butter in large saucepan over low heat. Blend in flour and seasonings. Cook over low heat, stirring until mixture is smooth and bubbly. Remove from heat. Stir in broth and cream. Heat to boiling, stirring constantly. Boil and stir 1 minute. Stir in spaghetti, chicken, and mushrooms. Pour into ungreased 2-quart casserole. Sprinkle with cheese. Bake uncovered 30 minutes or until bubbly. To brown, place briefly under broiler.

Chicken Casserole
Serves 12.

2 cans cream of chicken soup
1½ cups mayonnaise
2 t. salt
2 small packages sliced almonds
2 cups diced celery
2 T. minced onions
2 cups cooked rice
2 T. lemon juice
3-4 cups cooked chicken
6 hard-cooked eggs
American cheese (grated)
crushed potato chips

Mix and cook the first 6 ingredients for a short time, until hot. Add rice, lemon juice, and chicken and mix. Top with sliced eggs, cheese, and chips. Bake at 350° for 45 minutes.

Ham, Broccoli, Cheese Pie

Six generous servings.

2 cups cooked ham, cut into ½-inch
　　cubes
1 package frozen, chopped broccoli
2 cups shredded Swiss cheese
3 T. chopped onion
1 cup scalded milk
3 slightly beaten eggs
salt (very lightly) and pepper to taste
1 unbaked 9- or 10-inch pastry shell

Cook the broccoli according to the package directions. Drain. Spread ½ of the ham, broccoli, and cheese in the shell. Repeat the layers and spread chopped onion on top. Gradually stir milk into the beaten eggs, add the seasonings and pour over the top of the filled pie. Bake in 450° oven for 10 minutes. Lower heat to 325° and bake 25 minutes or longer (until center is firm).

Sausage Biscuits

These are very easy to make and delicious for breakfast. The amount of ingredients you will need will depend on the number you will be serving. Use a tube biscuit or your favorite recipe and cook according to the directions. While the biscuits are cooking fry the sausage in patties. Drain the patties (when done) and place them in between the pieces of hot biscuits.

Sausage Cheese Quiche

Makes 6 large servings.

Pastry for 1 crust 9-inch pie
8 ounces pork sausage (bulk)
4 hard-cooked eggs, chopped
1 cup shredded Swiss cheese
1 cup shredded Cheddar cheese
3 beaten eggs
1¼ cups milk
½ t. salt
dash of pepper

Line a 9-inch pie pan with pastry. Do not prick the pie. Bake in a 350° oven for only 10 minutes. Cook the sausage and drain well. Sprinkle the hard-cooked eggs in the bottom of the pie shell. Top with the sausage (crumbled) and cheeses. Combine the beaten eggs, milk, salt, and pepper; pour over the other mixture. Bake in a 350° oven for 30 to 35 minutes or until set. Let stand a few minutes before serving. May be cut in small wedges as an appetizer.

He who is not busy being born is busy dying.

Ham Loaf

Eight servings.

2 pounds ground ham
1 pound ground pork
2 eggs
1 can crushed pineapple
1 box corn flakes

Mix above ingredients all together in form of a loaf. Bake in oven 1 hour at 350°, with water in bottom of pan to keep from burning.

Miniature Ham and Swiss Cheese Sandwiches

Ham, sliced very thin
Swiss cheese slices, cut in half
½ cup margarine
2 T. mustard
1 T. poppy seeds
6 small hamburger buns

Place the ham and cheese on each bun. Melt the margarine and add the mustard and poppy seeds. Brush the sauce on each bun (being as generous as your taste desires). Wrap in foil and heat in the oven 20 to 30 minutes at 325° or until the cheese is melted.

Egg and Muffin

Makes 6.

3 whole wheat English muffins, split
6 slices Cheddar cheese
6 thin ham slices
butter
6 fried eggs

Place split muffins lightly buttered in oven with pieces of cheese covered with ham. Keep in the oven so that the cheese melts and the ham gets warm. While those are heating fry the eggs in a little grease on top of the stove. When the eggs are cooked to the degree of doneness desired place an egg on each muffin (with the ham and cheese). These may be kept warm in the oven while you finish fixing the rest of the breakfast.

Ham Glaze

1 t. ground clove
3-ounce package raspberry Jello
3 T. honey

Rub ham surface with cloves. Put ham on foil in pan. Pour powdered Jello over ham, then pour on honey. Fold foil securely around ham. Bake at 350° for 1½ hours.

Pork Chop Dinner

4 to 8 pork chops
salt, pepper, and flour mixture
3 or 4 large potatoes
2 or 3 onions
1 can beef broth or vegetable soup
1 can water

Roll pork chops in the flour mixture; fry until brown. In a baking dish put a layer of potatoes, a layer of onions, salt, and pepper. Place the chops on top and pour on the beef broth or vegetable soup, and water. Cover and bake at 375° about 50 minutes. Uncover and brown.

Pork Cutlets Mornay

1 pound pork cutlets
1 beaten egg
½ cup bread crumbs

Sauce:
2 T. butter, melted
2 T. flour
salt
pepper
⅛ t. nutmeg
1 cup cream
⅛ t. cayenne pepper
1 cup sharp cheese, shredded
½ cup grated Cheddar cheese

Flatten cutlets. Season and dip in beaten egg and bread crumbs. Fry in hot fat until golden brown on both sides. Reduce heat, add small amount of water, cover tightly and braise until tender—about 30 minutes. Cover with sauce Mornay (made by combining sauce ingredients). Sprinkle with ½ cup grated cheese and paprika. Place under broiler until hot and bubbly.

Sausage Skillet
Serves 6.

1 pound pork sausage meat
¼ cup chopped onion
3 cups cooked rice
2 cups tomatoes
½ cup chili sauce

Cook rice according to package directions. In skillet, fry crumbled sausage meat and onion until lightly browned. Stir with spatula to fry uniformly. Drain off fat. Add cooked rice, tomatoes, and chili sauce. Blend thoroughly. Cover. Cook over a low flame for 30 minutes.

Tuna Macaroni Casserole

2 cups cooked macaroni

1 can cream of mushroom soup

½ cup milk

1 7-ounce can of tuna

¼ cup minced onion

½ cup shredded cheese

grated cheese

Mix cream of mushroom soup with milk. Add tuna (drained and flaked), minced onion, and shredded cheese. Add this to the drained, cooked macaroni. Sprinkle some grated cheese on top. (Refrigerate if you care to, but remove ½ hour before putting it in the oven.) Bake about ½ hour or a little longer at 350°.

Crab Imperial a la Maryland

½ cup medium white sauce

1 egg, separated

2 T. mayonnaise

2 t. Worcestershire sauce

1 t. mustard

1 t. salt

dash of pepper

1½ cups flaked, fresh crab meat

1 egg, lightly beaten

3 T. butter

bread crumbs

Preheat oven to 450°. Grease crab shells or individual casseroles. Combine white sauce, egg yolk, mayonnaise, mustard, pepper, and salt. Combine crab meat and beaten egg; stir into sauce. Beat egg white until stiff (but not dry); fold into crab mixture. Divide into sixths and put in shells or casseroles. Sprinkle with bread crumbs and dot with butter. Bake 10 to 15 minutes.

Seafood Fancy

¾ cup chopped green pepper
¾ cup chopped onion
1 cup diced celery
1 cup crab meat
1 cup diced shrimp
½ t. salt
dash of pepper
1 t. Worcestershire sauce
1 cup mayonnaise

1 cup bread crumbs
2 T. melted butter

Combine vegetables, crab meat, shrimp, salt, pepper, Worcestershire sauce, and mayonnaise. Place in greased 1-quart casserole or 6 baking shells. Toss crumbs in butter and sprinkle over the top. Bake at 350° for 30 minutes or until hot and crumbs are brown.

"For all that has been, thanks;
For all that is yet to be, yes."
—Dag Hammarskjold

Hot Seafood Souffle

Serves 12.

8 slices bread (or more if slices are
   small)
2 cups crab or shrimp
½ cup mayonnaise
1 medium onion, chopped
1 green pepper, chopped
1 cup celery, chopped
3 cups milk
4 eggs
1 can mushroom soup
1 cup grated cheese
paprika

Dice half of bread and cover the bottom of a 13x9x2-inch baking dish with it. Mix the crab or shrimp, mayonnaise, onion, green pepper, celery and spread over the diced bread. Trim crust from the remaining bread and place over the mixture. Mix eggs and milk together and pour over the top. Place in the refrigerator and leave over night.

Bake 15 minutes in oven preheated to 325°. Remove from the oven and spoon the soup over the top, sprinkle grated cheese over all and then paprika on top of the cheese. Bake one hour (or a little longer) in a 325° oven.

Shrimp Creole

Serves 2—generously.

¾ cup chopped onion
1 clove garlic, pressed or minced
1 medium green pepper, finely
 chopped
½ cup finely chopped celery
2 T. butter
1 8-ounce can tomato sauce
½ cup water
1 bay leaf, crushed
1 t. minced parsley
½ t. salt
⅛ t. pepper
1 7-ounce package frozen shrimp,
 thawed, or 1 small can shrimp

In medium skillet, saute onion, garlic, green pepper, and celery in butter about 5 minutes, or until tender. Remove from heat; stir in tomato sauce, water, bay leaf, parsley, salt, and pepper. Simmer 10 minutes. Add additional water if needed. Add shrimp. Bring mixture to a boil; cook covered over medium heat 5 minutes. Serve over white rice.

These are the good old days.

Egg Foo Yung (China)

Four servings.

¼ pound cooked chicken
¼ pound cooked shrimp
4 mushrooms
8 green onion
1 stalk celery
5 eggs
½ t. salt
½ cup bean sprouts
3-4 T. peanut oil

1. *Coarsely chop chicken, shrimp, mushrooms.*
2. *Mince green onions, celery.*
3. *Beat eggs; blend in salt.*
4. *Stir in chicken, shrimp, mushrooms, onions, celery, bean sprouts.*
5. *Heat ½ tablespoon oil in 8-inch fry pan over medium-high heat; reduce heat to medium.*
6. *Pour ¼ cup egg mixture into fry pan; cook 1 minute on each side (should be lightly browned); keep warm in 200° oven; repeat until all batter is used; add more oil as needed.*
7. *Serve with Foo Yung Sauce.*

A

Au gratin—A browned covering of bread crumbs usually mixed with butter or cheese.

B

Bake—Cook in the oven.

Barbecue—Roast meat on a grill over hot coals, periodically basting it with a sauce.

Baste—Spoon liquid or fat over food while it is cooking.

Beat—Mix fast with spoon or beater to make smooth.

Blanch—Plunge into boiling water, then into cold water.

Blend—Mix ingredients until smooth.

Boil—Cook in liquid so hot that bubbles break on the surface.

Bouillon—A clear meat broth.

Broil—Cook directly under heating unit.

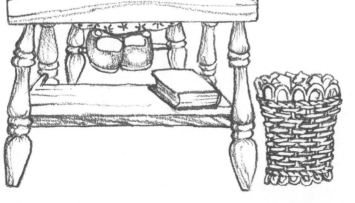

C

Canapé—Small piece of fried or toasted bread topped with sea food, cheese, or meat.

Caramelize—Melt granulated sugar over medium heat to brown syrup.

Chop—Cut in small pieces with knife, scissors, or chopper.

Combine—Mix ingredients

Consommé—Clear broth made with meat and/or chicken.

Cream—Rub shortening against bowl with spoon or beat with mixer until light and creamy.

Cut in—Mix fat into flour mixture using a fork, two knives, or a pastry blender.

D

Dice—Cut into small cubes.

Dredge—Coat heavily with flour.

E

Entrée—Chief dish of the main course which is a meat, poultry, fish, or meat substitute.

Eclair—Oblong shape of cream puff paste filled with custard or whipped cream.

F

Filet—Boneless, thin strip of lean meat or fish.

Fold in—Cut down through, across bottom, up and over top, doing it over and over again until ingredients are blended.

French fry—Cook in hot fat deep enough to float the food.

Fry—Panfry in small amount of fat.

G

Garnish—The extra that makes food look so good—a cherry or parsley.

Goulash—Thick Hungarian meat stew flavored with vegetables.

H

Hollandaise—Sauce made of butter and egg yolks with seasoning such as lemon juice or vinegar.

Hors d'oeuvres—Variety of delightful appetizers.

K

Knead—Work the dough with pressing, folding, and stretching motions. May also be pressing dough with heel of hand.

M

Marinate—Let food stand in dressing mixture (such as French) to give added flavor.

Meringue—Mixture of stiffly beaten egg whites and sugar—usually for pie topping.

Mince—Chop or cut into small pieces.

Mix—Stir ingredients together.

P

Pare—Cut away outside skin as from fruits and vegetables.

Peel—Strip off outside covering as from a banana.

Petits fours—Little iced cakes cut into fancy designs and frosted decoratively.

Pit—Take out seeds.

Poach—Cook by using simmering (not boiling) water or other liquid.

Preheat—Turning on oven in time for it to be at right temperature when you have food ready to put in.

R

Relish—Food that is highly flavored and used with other food.

S

Sauté—Brown in small amount of fat in skillet.

Scald—Heat milk to just below boiling point until you see tiny bubbles around the edges.

Sear—Brown surface quickly.

Simmer—Cook in liquid over very low heat. Bubbles are lazylike.

Stew—Cook slowly in small amount of liquid for long time.

Stir—Mix with a spoon.

T

Torte—Rich cake, usually made from crumbs, eggs, sugar, and nuts.

Tortilla—Thin round Mexican food made from cornmeal and hot water.

Toss—Lightly mix ingredients without mashing them.

W

Whip—Whipping adds air through rich cream or egg whites until light and fluffy. You simply beat rapidly.